Secrets of Nature
FROM B-Z

DR. TUGLER

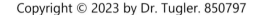

To order additional copies of this book, contact:
Xlibris
844-714-8691
www.Xlibris.com
Orders@Xlibris.com

ISBN: Softcover   979-8-3694-1187-2
         EBook   979-8-3694-1186-5

Print information available on the last page

Rev. date: 11/22/2023

CONTENTS

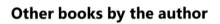

Other books by the author

Secrets of Nature from A-Z
Secrets of Nature from B-Z

Coming soon: *Secrets of Nature from C-Z*

Dear parents,

You could read this story with your smart, curious children who are interested in investigation, science, and nature. Teachers could use it in class to read and analyze different situations with the students. This story is for young adults and others, especially those interested in science, solving problems, and investigation.

To all readers: This book could help improve your knowledge of different realms of nature and sharpen your intellectual skills.

In the books you will get acquainted with space pirates and students of Galactic University, smart octopi and even smarter whales, disputing chemists, and oil-miners! These and other book characters will take you to space and underground, to the North Pole and to the African desert, to mountains and waterfalls, to warm snow and cold fire, and even to listen to an echo. All these fantastic adventures are waiting for you in the series.

Let's continue with letter
B

BALLOON

A passenger balloon is a flying apparatus made of strong yet light material filled with gas.

Once, two friends, Idler and Curious, were walking together in a park. Idler, as usual, was wasting time doing nothing, just staring around. It looked like there was nothing that could really impress him. Curious, on the other hand, was eager to know and to learn about all things that seemed unfamiliar or mysterious.

As they were walking, they saw a hot-air balloon about to start flying. While Idler was staring at it, Curious began to wonder why the balloon rises.

Idler: What difference does it make?! The balloon goes up whether you understand why or not!

Curious: You don't understand! There's some kind of mystery here.

Idler: What's the mystery? Everyone knows balloons go up. Besides I have the answer. The balloon goes up because of solar energy.

Curious: How could solar energy have anything to do with it?

Idler: Why not? The sun always shines on the balloon, so it gives the balloon its heat energy, doesn't it? And I suppose you think it moves because of the wind!

Curious: Wait, wait! We're talking about why it goes up, not how and why it moves in the sky. When the balloon is in the sky, of course the wind helps it move. The balloon sails with the wind. And by the way, the balloon is painted light gray to reflect the sun's rays away from it, so solar energy cannot be the answer here.

Idler: Why would anyone want to keep the sun's rays away from the balloon?

Curious: They are so hot that the balloon could become too hot and burn up. But that still doesn't explain why the balloon rises!

Idler: I think that the balloon goes up because of the potential energy it gathers when being filled with gas.

Curious: You're just using fancy words you heard once at school. And by the way, you are forgetting about Archimedes' Principle!

Idler: Archimedes' Principle?! Who's using the fancy words now?

Curious: Archimedes' Principle states that an object partly or totally placed in a liquid or gas

is buoyed up or supported by a force equal to the weight of the liquid or gas it displaces. The lesser the density, the lesser the mass of the balloon, the lesser the force of gravity which pulls the balloon down. So, the balloon goes up faster because it is lighter, and that is why they fill balloons with gases that have low densities. I suppose they use hydrogen most often.

Idler: Hydrogen? But it's not that safe. It could explode. And I think I remember now that helium is used sometimes. Helium is an inert gas. It won't explode.

Curious: Hmmm. And what is an inert gas?

Idler: An inert gas is a gas that usually does not combine with other substances, so there is no danger of getting an explosive combination. I hear these gases are very hard to find. They are very rare. They are even called noble gases because of that. Like how it's rare to find members of the nobility.

Curious: They are called noble gases because they don't react with other elements, like how nobles didn't want to associate with the common folk in the olden days. Besides, helium

is heavier than hydrogen. Hydrogen is the lightest gas, right?

Idler: Well, you are right! I think because of that they use either one of these two gases, depending on the situation. If they want to go higher, they might risk using hydrogen.

Curious: Gases... forces... Wait, we are forgetting about energy!

Idler: Right. We still haven't figured out what energy is involved here.

While the friends continued their discussion, the balloon flew up and disappeared in the clouds. Neither of them could understand what energy enabled the balloon to rise. And what about you? Do you have any suggestions that would help Idler and Curious?

If you didn't find the answer to the main question of this mysterious story, we can help you. Do you remember how Idler said: I think that the balloon goes up because of the potential energy it gathers when being filled with gas.

Dear parents,

For your children to understand this story clearly, we prepared investigative questions and answers for them. You could use the answers if you need them to discuss "Balloon" with your children. But first ask them to try to find the answers in the story.

Dear Children! Are you a detective? Find the **a**nswers to the questions in the text.

Questions

1. What is a passenger balloon?
2. What force pulls passenger balloons to the earth?
3. Why does a passenger balloon go up?
4. What kind of energy do we get from the sun?
5. What helps move passenger balloons in the sky?
6. Why are passenger balloons painted light gray?
7. Why can passenger balloons burn up?
8. What forces act on a passenger balloon?
9. When can passenger balloons go faster?
10. Which gas does not explode?
11. Which gases do not combine with other substances?
12. Which gas is the lightest?

Answers

1. A passenger balloon is a flying apparatus made of strong yet light material and is filled with gas.
2. The force of gravity pulls the balloon down to earth.
3. Archimedes' Principle states that a body partly or totally placed in a liquid or gas is buoyed up or supported by a force equal to the weight of the liquid or gas it displaces.
4. Solar energy.
5. When the balloon is in the sky, the wind helps it move. The balloon sails with the wind.
6. The balloon is painted a light gray to reflect the sun's rays away from the balloon.
7. The balloon could become too hot and burn up.
8. The force of gravity pulls down the balloon. The balloon is supported by a force equal to the weight of the liquid or gas it displaces.
9. The lesser the density, the lesser the mass of the balloon, the lesser the force of gravity which pulls down the balloon. So, the balloon goes up faster because it is lighter.
10. Inert gas. Helium is used sometimes. Helium is an inert gas.

11. An inert gas is a gas that usually does not combine with other substances, so there is no danger of getting an explosive combination.
12. They use hydrogen most often.

Glossary

1. Archimedes' Principle: can explain why an object floats in the air or water.
2. Balloon: small brightly colored rubber bag that can be blown up, used as a toy, or decoration for parties.
3. Passenger balloon: a large bag of strong, light material filled with gas or heated air so that it can float in the air.
4. Density: the ratio of the amount of matter (the mass) to the space into which the matter is packed (its volume); any given volume of helium is heavier than the same volume of hydrogen.
5. Energy: the capacity to perform work.
6. Solar energy: heat and other kinds of energy that comes from the sun.
7. Heat energy: can heat an object.
8. Potential energy: the stored energy of an object in terms of its condition or position with respect to the other objects.
9. Force: physical power of movement that changes or may produce changes in an object on which it acts.
10. Force of gravity: the force with which Earth pulls on a body or any kind of object with mass.
11. Gas: one of the three substances of the body (gas, liquid, solid).
12. Hydrogen: a gas that is a simple substance (element) without color or smell and burns very easily.
13. Helium: a gas that is a simple substance (element) which does not burn, and is used in airships and some kinds of lights.
14. Inert gas: gas, like helium, that does not react chemically when combined with other substances.
15. Liquid: one of the three substances of the body (gas, liquid, solid) which flows and has no fixed shape.
16. Reflection: when a body throws back heat, light, sound, or an image. It's a phenomenon where rays are thrown back from the surface of any object.

Dear Readers! Now you know **why a passenger balloon flies.** Stay with us and you will be smarter. We wish you good luck in your investigation of nature's laws in our next story starting with the letter **B**.

BALL

Mermaid and Merman were watching people do experiments with liquid, and decided to repeat these experiments, or maybe even try to improve them since they are experts in all things water. For the first experiment, they used a glass of mercury and steel balls.

Mermaid: You see, Merman, the steel ball is floating in the mercury.

Merman: And what will happen if you drop the ball in water? I'm more interested in what happens to the ball in the water.

Mermaid: What do you think? Let's do an experiment in another glass... You see, it's sinking. And look! Now I am pouring water on the steel ball floating in the mercury. What do you think will happen?

Merman: It will sink more.

Mermaid: Why do you think that?

Merman: Because the water is pressing it. Do you know what kind of force this is? Yesterday, I was swimming deeper in the ocean than usual and I barely survived because of the water pressure. Nobody can live there. Even the fish with "protruding eyes" live higher. Water is very powerful!

Mermaid: But Archimedes' force pushes the ball in both glasses.

Merman: Well then the ball will go up and float! Please, would you stop annoying me? I am very busy and have no time for your pranks! Stop bothering me! Why don't you go disturb the real people?

Mermaid: But you saw that the steel ball sank in the water.

Merman: Now I'm completely confused! I always knew I shouldn't talk to Mermaids.

Mermaid: I'm not trying to confuse you; when you add water to the mercury, the ball will float a little above the mercury. Do you understand?

Merman: You know, I've noticed that the submarine, when lowered onto the muddy bottom of the ocean, sometimes has great difficulty breaking away from the bottom of the ocean, even if the ballast tanks (the chambers that fill up with water when the ship is submerged and completely release the water if it needs to float up) are free of water. Have you seen this?

Mermaid: Of course I've seen it! I always try to help them in those situations, pulling them up out of the bottom, since they could drown. I feel bad for them!

Merman: Of course. The people will say that I drowned them! But I know that nature's laws are acting, which I cannot change. Do you think I'm right?

Mermaid: Obviously. You're always right, even when you're wrong.

Merman: Mermaid, are you being sarcastic or are you praising me?

Mermaid: Of course I'm praising you!

Merman: Excellent, please continue complimenting me.

Mermaid: When the boat is firmly pressed to the ocean's muddy bottom so that there's no water between the boat and the ocean floor, there is no water pressure on the bottom of the submarine, therefore there is no upward force. The water pressure is on top of the submarine, and together with the submarine's weight, it is pressed down into the ocean floor.

Merman: Wonderful! The people who blame me for this crime should investigate your claim by doing an experiment to understand how it actually works.

Mermaid: What kind of experiment could they do?

Merman: You take a piece of wax and throw it into the water. What do you think will happen to it in the water?

Mermaid: I know that the wax will float.

Merman: Well, if you first melt the wax, pour it in an empty glass and let it harden, it will be flat and smooth. On top, put another smooth and flat rectangle of wax and carefully pour water on the top of the wax so that there is no water between the hardened piece of wax and the rectangular piece of wax. What will happen then?

Mermaid: I assume that the piece of wax on top will stick to the bottom of the glass, even though wax usually floats in water...

Merman: See! I'm telling you that I'm not guilty! They drown by themselves because their captains didn't study physics!

Mermaid: Ha-ha! In this case you're right! The water does not go under the wax, and the water just pushes the wax down. Just like with the submarine, which could not float up.

Merman: That's what I was trying to explain with my story and experiment. Where do you think it will be easier for a human to float, a freshwater lake or the saltwater ocean?

Mermaid: In the ocean of course, since the density of ocean water is greater than the density of lake water. However, people are more afraid of the ocean or the sea because of the endlessness of the ocean and sink from fear.

Merman: Yeah, yeah of course, density of water... I help the people, not the water!

Mermaid: No, I help the people more! They are less scared of me than you!

Merman: Fine! Let's not argue! It doesn't matter, we work together!

Mermaid: Agreed!

The **Merman** and the **Mermaid** swam away on their own business. What, didn't you realize, my dear readers, that the stories of the dwellers of the ocean and sea are, in fact, close to reality?

Question: What will happen to the steel ball in the mercury when water is poured on top?

Answer: If you didn't find the answer to the main question of this mysterious story, we can help you. The steel ball will float up a little because mercury is also a liquid, so the pressure of the water acts on the mercury.

Dear parents,

For your children to understand this story clearly, we prepared investigative questions and answers for them. You could use the answers if you need them to discuss "Ball" with your children. But first ask them to try to find the answers in the story.

Dear Children! Are you a detective? Find the **a**nswers to the questions in the text.

Questions

1. What is potential energy?
2. Why does the ball float in the mercury but sink in the water?
3. What is Archimedean Force, which pushes the ball up?
4. What is a submarine? Can you draw a picture of it?
5. Why does the submarine, when lowered onto the muddy bottom of the ocean, sometimes have great difficulty breaking away from the bottom of the ocean, even if the ballast tanks are empty?
6. What is wax?
7. Why does the captain of the submarine not know physics?
8. Are the Merman and the Mermaid real people who live in the ocean?

Answers

1. Potential energy is the energy that an object has when lifted above the Earth.
2. Mercury has a larger density than water.
3. Archimedes' Force is the force that pushes an object out of a liquid.
4. A submarine is a ship that is designed to travel underwater.
5. The water pressure pushes the submarine down into the muddy bottom of the ocean, since there is no water under the submarine.
6. Wax is the substance that makes up candles.
7. The captain of the submarine does not know physics because he put the submarine onto the muddy floor of the ocean.
8. No, the Merman and the Mermaid are fictional characters from a fairytale.

Glossary

1. Archimedes' Principle: can explain why the body floats in the air or the water.
2. Force: physical power of movement that changes or may produce changes in the acceleration of the body on which it acts.
3. Force of gravity: makes things fall to Earth or another planet.
4. Liquid: one of the three substances of the body: gas, liquid, solid. Water is a liquid, which flows, is wet, and has no fixed shape.

Dear Readers! Now you know **why a steel ball floats or sinks.** Stay with us and you will be smarter. We wish you good luck in your investigation of nature's laws in our next story starting with the letter **B**.

BOATS

Once upon a time, a captain and a first mate came to a pier. Silently they were watching the waves and listening to seagulls. They saw two similar boats approaching the pier. The boats were pulled toward the shore with the help of two ropes. One end of the first boat's rope was tied to the dock. One end of the other boat's rope was pulled by a sailor who was standing on the pier. Two men, one on each boat, pulled the other end of each rope. All three, both the men on the boats and the sailor, were pulling with the same strength.

Captain: Which boat will get to the shore first, do you think?

First mate: The one which is pulled by two people.

Captain: Oh, you inexperienced youth! You will see they will come in at the same time! Want to bet?

First mate: Sure!

Captain: What will we bet for?

First mate: Your captain's cap.

Captain: So you will get mine, or I will get yours.

First mate: Agreed.

Captain: You probably don't remember Newton's third law. You are going to lose!

First mate: What does Newton's third law have to do with this?

Captain: Oh, it just explains everything in this situation.

First mate: I do remember that the mutual actions of two bodies upon each other are always equal and are directly opposite. If you push a stone, the stone pushes you back. If a horse draws a cart, the cart will equally draw the horse backwards.

Captain: So the thing is that the pillar is also "pulling" the rope. Its "strength" is equal to that of the sailor who pulls or, more accurately, holds the rope while standing on the pier. As long as the forces applied to all ends of all ropes are the same, both boats are in identical situations. Meaning that they would reach the shore at the same time.

First mate: Your interpretation of Newton's laws is wrong. You just don't understand them!

Captain: And why is that?

First mate: The man on the second boat and the sailor are both pulling the rope while only one sailor is pulling on the first boat. So, the second boat will move two times faster.

Captain: For it to move twice as fast, the force applied by the two sailors should be twice as much, and we know that they are the same.

First mate: I'm starting to get confused. Maybe you're right...

Captain: Just wait a moment and we will see who's right and who's wrong. I am just afraid that...

First mate: What are you afraid of? Losing?

Captain: No, of course not. I am just afraid that your cap is going to be too small for me!

Bending over the pier's railing, the two "old salts" strained to get a clear picture of the boats, mentally encouraging "their" boat to go faster, while also imagining how they would look with each other's caps.

Answer: If you didn't find the answer to the main question of this mysterious story, we can help you. The two boats will reach the shore at the same time.

Dear parents,

For your children to understand this story clearly, we prepared investigative questions and answers for them. You could use the answers if you need them to discuss "Boats" with your children. But first ask them to try to find the answers in the story.

Dear Children! Are you a detective? Find the **a**nswers to the questions in the text.

Questions

1. What was the bet about?
2. What did they bet for?
3. What is Newton's third law?
4. Why was the interpretation of Newton's laws given by the captain wrong?
5. Who is right?
6. Who is wrong?
7. Who is the winner?

Answers

1. Which boat will get to the shore first.
2. The captain's cap.
3. The mutual actions of two bodies upon each other are always equal and are directly opposite. If you push a stone, the stone pushes you back. If a horse draws a cart, the cart will equally draw the horse backwards.
4. The man on the second boat and the sailor are both pulling the rope while only one sailor is pulling on the first boat. So, the second boat will move two times faster.
5. Captain. The pillar is also "pulling" the rope. Its "strength" is equal to that of the sailor who pulls or, more accurately, holds the rope while standing on the pier. As long as the forces applied to all ends of all ropes are the same, both boats are in identical situations. Meaning that they would reach the shore at the same time.
6. First mate. The man on the second boat and the sailor are both pulling the rope while only one sailor is pulling on the first boat. So, the second boat will move two times faster.
7. Captain.

Glossary

1. Captain: the person in charge of a boat

2. First mate: the captain's right-hand man who is in charge of the boat when the captain isn't there

3. Pillar: a wooden pole that boats are tied to

4. Pier: where boats are docked

5. Force: physical power of movement that changes or may produce changes in a body on which it acts.

6. Newton's laws: The first law states that an object will not change its motion unless a force acts on it. The second law says that as more force is applied to a body, it accelerates more. The third law states that for every action, there is an equal and opposite reaction.

Dear Readers! From the previous stories, you know about the hot-air **balloons,** the effect of Archimedes' Principle on a **ball**, and the connection of **boats** to Newton's laws. Stay with us and you will be smarter. We wish you good luck in your investigation of nature's laws in the next book called

SECRETS of NATURE
from
C-Z

The ability to speak, to state
one's thoughts clearly, to
prove a point is not innate...
but this ability can be very
important in everyday
conversation and in
winning arguments.
To help you learn how to
argue effectively and answer
your partner's questions
clearly is the aim of this
book. You will find a
variety of dialogues inside
in which different characters
try to prove their point of view
on different subjects basing
their arguments and statements
on the laws of science.

Printed in the United States
by Baker & Taylor Publisher Services